DON'T PANIC

M. A. MORTÉN

DON'T PANIC

"When the power of love,
overcomes the love of power,
the world will know Peace."
– Jimi Hendrix

Publisher:
BoD – Books on Demand, Helsinki, Finland
Manufacturer:
BoD – Books on Demand, Norderstedt, Germany
ISBN: 978-952-339-310-3

I

FICTION MADE REALITY

MEGA

I am Mega.
My Dad's the Alpha.
My Mom's the Omega.

I am a Gem.

They're the Jewels; stars and the
universe.

UNDER JUPITERS RULE

Walking under the rule of Jupiter;
covering life like it's always
November.

Living in the middle of death and
flying arrows.

When I saw a shooting star
I made a wish, an opinion, belief
and an idea.

Waiting for the proposal;
possibility, even a suggestion.

FICTION MADE REALITY

All those fantasies
Adventures in the wild

Heroes defeating villains

What was once make-belief
now had won

All that fun.

Fiction made reality
by a wish of the one

Like Miyazaki had a son

The second run
now has begun.

OTHERWORLDLY COLOURS

In a blink of an eye
Two or three heartbeats
And switch of a light

Otherworldly colours so bright,
might I even be frighten the
height.

All I need is a breath of fresh air
You know, a way somewhere.

YOU ARE

It can be both, a curse and a
blessing to be a healer.

You're a thievish heart stealer
World creator.

You're a magnificent dreamer
Mind carver.

You're a glamorous laugher
Emotion engineer.

MATHEMATICAL SOLUTION

Hollow shaped mathematical
solution to love
Has to be calculated

Temper and nature
Has to be just right

It can't thrive in a dark and scary
atmosphere

Also by adding too much sugar in
the water, it becomes poison

Only way to survive is to become
equal.

BLOOD DROPS

In the darkness of space; blood
drops floated like soap bubbles in
the sky.

Frozen and ready to comprise life

There was something about you.
Your instantly visible eye color
told me.

I COULD

I could see it in your eyes, that
you've heard the silent scream.

Most heart crippling voiceless
sound, the eerie bird in the mist.

I could feel it in your touch, that
you've felt the cold hands.

Those lonely, faceless fingers
The hazy drunks in the bliss

I could hear it in your absence,
that you've scared the warm
smiles.

Misty new affectionate
friendships: fiery moments; yet to
be experienced.

BOW OF ENVY

Someone bended the bow of envy
the jealousy arrow ready
soul string set to shoot.

Why didn't I see
your eyes could have told me
more than anyone would?

Fired from unknown roots
nobody even moved
poison spite hit the heart.

CHECKMATE

Checkmate, it's the end.
How does it come to this, no more
blood to spill?

Many furious plans with vivid
details, methods to get that job
done, soldiers fall, horses gets
eaten and towers crumple.

Lady Queen in red velvet lures the
rest of them in, the king gets them
in line, there's nothing you could
have done.

Mouth speaks the misunderstood
words, all heard to be crazy,
awkward, embarrassing failure

Sometimes I just sit and fucking
ponder what happened, am I not
allowed to marvel!

THE FUTURE

Despite all effort,
Future is unknown again.

It hurts like hell when I hit the
ground.

There I lay, on the pit of nothing,
clawing myself bloody, when I try
to see.

With no effort, time flows to the
unknown.

It heals me like water, when I rise
again.

II

SHAMEFUL MYSTICISM

SHAMEFUL MYSTICISM

Hey, there is a clock in the wall to
keep you calm.

Heart beats towards
understanding.

Inward eye blinks, devouring
deadly cravings and suffering.

Oh don't look so blind,
at least there's a collective reality
to soothe your soul.

Release your true and full nature.

There is no shameful mysticism
when you are crying of
compassion, fail trying to acquire
a skill or go silent when hearing
words of wisdom.

THIS AND THAT

Remember when we all use to
share the same Coca-Cola bottle.

No one cared if you didn't even
shower when we were all friends.

Now it's all snapchat this and
WhatsApp that
ringtones and no doorbells.

Freedom lives through that
Facebook stare
personal interaction, I think it is
dead.

SWEET SHADOWS

Fiery violent light, almighty love
sometimes it seems to burn out;
locked away in hearts maximum
security prison.

You are luring.

Nice night,
How you hold on with all you
might

Dreamy darkness, how you
swallow me like the ocean.

Sweet shadows, how you try to
imitate the light.

DON'T STOP

All this poisonous self-love
choking the people

No more mister nice guys
poor or rich.

Every man, woman and child for
themselves

Run, they'll tell you, run to the
hills and don't stop.

Twisted ways we stay young and
forget.

TARANTULA HEART

It has my tarantula heart

Lizard mind
Slouch lion body

Try and have dreams of a penguin
and dance.

CHRYSTAL BALL

I don't know where I am going;
half the times don't know what I'm
doing.

Dwelling in the frozen past;
replaying it on minds crystal ball,
safe and out of reach.

BEST FRIENDS AT CHECK

The world has no place for my
troubles.

My world has no room for hate.
I simply cannot take you to face it.
I'd rather show you love and light
then it's even fun to fight.

Maybe we can be both right.

Troubles and hate don't go out;
lingering between heart and the
brain, trying to lift a ride in my
breath.

DAYS IN THE DARK

Dirty dishes in the sink;
washed away too many painful
memories down thinking of you.
I force and I fight, I lost too many
days to the dark.

Distorted divinity on the wall,
scrolled many bogus news all the
way.

Speaking the truth; I shy and I cry,
I listen too many lies at the
theater.

Dystopian dreams in the brink;
rewind many poor mistakes in my
head.

Feeling the ache; I try and I shy, I
walk too many miles in the search
of you.

III

MAGIGAL
FIRES

WATER

I am fire in the water.
Traveler in this particular nebula

Loves archer under the forest
trees, suns messenger bathing in
the moonlight

A blip
Only a glimpse
A photon of light

I don't wanna fight
I don't want to envy
I just love water

Can we share our problems
care for one another?

FLAMES

Our bright yellow flame of love
was hanging in the air
trying to grasp the concept of
infinity.

Our particles completely burned
away.

There is just enough oxygen to let
my blue flame to occur and my
tears flow carbon black.

THE ELVIS

Sometimes you just wanna sing
like Elvis and be like,

'Loving you makes my heart drop
down, down to your arms; oh you
are making me crumble.'

Then a noise from the street
wakes you up from your daily
slumber.

75%

The glass is 75% full
wallet full of notes
still walking, try smiling

Experiences make you rich
Not money

Life is best before the end
please check the bottom.

MAD AS FICTION

A handful of fractured feelings
No words of wisdom

Just blissful intuition
wishful drinking

Rarely any thinking
And mad as fiction.

EVERY TIME

Every time I try to embrace the
darkness; the meridian sun
strikes, giving hope, where there is
none.

You shouldn't joke about it.

Every time I try to wake up in the
morning; buzz of the world
reminds me it was a dream.

An act on instinct, you could talk
about it.

SPIRIT GROTTO

Yes.

It is hard to believe, that an easy
solution is there in your complex
mind.

A spirit, in that long grass,
Deep river, in that dark grotto,
tells you what to, what not to.

So I listen.

HERE

Finally you are here.
You don't have to say you see.

I see the beginning of the biggest
smile, now that the voices and
the sounds are here.

It doesn't end on this spot.
Now it's time for you to make
them see.

I'm done and ready to disappear,
now stop running and start loving.

You are gonna take people with
you.
Time to start healing and
give your hand

Fade them troubles and be free.

LANTERNS IN THE TREES

The sunburn was nice in Hell
today, what else would they do
with our dead bodies

I think they toast champagne
glasses in the backroom

Costumes for the customers
Tombs for the living dead
Fumes of fluids exiting

Compound made of metal and ice

Lava current sizzling and the
lizards are running

I think they drink with that guy
from his golden horns.

WITHOUT

Searching for words that doesn't
exist

Explaining motions without a
color

Reminiscing an old memory
without the sound

Visioning things from the past and
searching the future without a
picture

Flowing in the now
Without clues about the effects

ALIEN BODY

You know, everybody knows it
today.

You are suffering too.
Oh, you're brave soul.

How does your heart sing in the
realm and speaks out, true.

You are quiet too.
Oh, your wounded heart.

How I forget that too soon in the
afternoon and seek out, true.

You are lonely too.
Oh, your alien body.

How did I get here too soon in the
light of the moon and hide out,
true.

IMPOSSIBILITY

How many dreams it kills when it
is said that something is not
possible

To every impossibility there has to
be a possible alternative proposal
or a new method of
implementation

If something is too big for your
head to realize, does not mean
that someone would not find
always something to say

Through which an impossible task
is easier to accomplish.

THE DOOR

I can only open the door, but
you have to make the choice.

I'm sorry you had to realize that
life is not a musical.

Sorry that you had to go through
all of it.

But you are a tough son of a witch,
I give you that.

HALL OF BROKEN DREAMS

In the hall of broken dreams
Pre-life's waiting room
echoed

"Why do I have to stay so long
after you've done your business?"
Misery asked from Death.

DEAD ARE WAKING UP

Some of them are waking up now
it echoes in their hearts, the sound
of trust.
Most of them are already dead
it glows from their smartphones
them swiping eerie lust.

All of them are unique and maybe
we really are crazy, visioning the
end for our laziness.
It's just, I wanna say babies; tell
me I'm insane, but the main thing
is love, loving hard the way you
are.

Most of them turn assholes
it shows no grace, tricking into
mindfucks.
Easy to move into your head, but
it's a long road to be moving into
your heart.

CRIME

Only the love for You

There are really bad things you
can do, really awful things
and really horrible too.

But there is no bigger crime in the
world, than that these poems
don't reveal your identity.

LABYRINTH

What once was a prison
or so thought the people
was actually the way out.

Maze of the mind
labyrinth of the body and
the movement of the hand
made the man make a plan.

BLACK MAGIC

What is this spell, your black
magic runs through my veins,
invisible force has its hold on me,
timeless, making me mindless.

I know this one and I realize here I
sit, in silence, in the darkness,

Numbing vigor effecting and
repeating, weightless, making me
dream.

Your green magic echoing in my
heart, visible and crystal clear
actions move me.

Hopeful, making me stitch my
wounds.

Sunny Day

It was a bright and sunny day
when I had to watch a demon
being born.

It was really the most beautiful
love story that turned real ugly in
the eyes of a total stranger.

Tragicomic pure infatuation
quickly turned to jealousy, and it
turned to hate, out of sadness and
hurt the demon was born.

TRICKSTER

There I said it
you know I'm the trickster
it's a tragicomedy.

Shadows and the sun's rays
the laughter and the rain
the thunder aching
And the mourning morning

My time

I don't always know what I'm
doing

I walk somewhere between love
and death.

SILENCE

All this time, you have been there,
this whole time, listening to the
mockery in your silence.

All this time you have been
everywhere, but nowhere to be
seen, traveling through the blood.

ONE CIGARETTE

Let me stay here on your arms
tonight, just this night.

I know, I'd better go now, still
have places to be.

Just one cigarette
To remember, where to continue
when we meet.

I don't want to forget, all say move
on, live and let go.

Exit is on the left, one more
cigarette?

IV

SUNNY TIMES IN VOID

TIME ZONE

When you are in love;
The past, present and the future
blends.

No time zone could tell you;
What time it is, you wouldn't even
care.

Does it rain or shine;
Dare I say you wouldn't even
notice?

All you could think are the lips;
Is it time to kiss?

I'M SORRY

I'm sorry.

To be a disappointment,
disposable, one cup, happy meal.

Recycled crushed can, half burned
old newspaper.

I'm sorry; to be disposable,
disappointment.

ON THE ROAD

Journey starts
loving fights and rights
dos and don'ts
cries and smiles.

On the road
Mr. and Mrs. rights
Rock 'n' roll and the break-ups
schools and hobbies.
On the road
Mornings and late nights
what you want and don't
real jazz and the friends you had.

On the road
Impulses and insecurity
what you had and didn't get
purple blues and the things you
have.
On the road
never know how long it lasts.

SAD HAPPY DANCE

Life is a sad happy dance.

They tell you everyone has a
chance.

I try to say I disagree; no-one
wants to understand.

Poor and the wicked, misbehaving,
broken, lost lassies

They all are part of this dance

Maybe in Machina cities
billionaires only know of trance.

10011

10110010110011101

Heads up, your body looks great,
stylesheets so sweet;
Links to heavenly treats

10110010110011101

Listen us your column content
reads fine, captions of actions,
titles to blood spilled tweets.

10110010110011101

Trust it, your sections moves nice
frustrations of classes, footers
don't move one after another.

THE WHITE NOISES

Only the white noises from the
battery operated radio whispers
measuring static distances.

Left here in case of radioactive
fallout; no use for the yearning.
It's a vortex.

There's a gap, a distance between.
Day runs ahead before the night
catches up.

Like the sun lost the moon;
Miles took you.

HISTORY

Remember that it's not about the
destination; it's all about the
journey.

If not at this moment, but latter
that you know why something was
the way it was

It's always a personal choice;
Do you wanna watch the world
burn, rather than write history.

YOU GOT MAIL

Just one lost soul.

I'd hate to spend my life.
I think you should live and I'm
dead inside.

You left but I can't forget,
Still staying by your side

Never seen anyone like you;
The same faces, reminding

I watch the sky and wait;
Rain will turn to sunshine.

Even if you don't answer my mail.

LOVE CAROUSEL

Love carousel starts to spin;
No one's gonna win
Enjoy 'till the end.

It doesn't matter how long or little
time you spend
Love is all, and it's up to you;
Do you break my heart and hurt
my feelings.

So bad, you get your revenge.

I know clichés are sweet in the
end, but then to me
You cease to exist.

You become the ghost in the
abyss; or go peacefully and
become immortal in my heart.

Love is all, all is love.

Don't be afraid of the envious and
the deceitful, all you need is your
love gun.

MAD DANCE

I almost danced, quickly cancelled
that.

Everything is going so fast, did I
miss my last chance?

Train is not on the track, someone
got mad.

I never had figured that.

Did I do wrong to things I never
had?

No Age

Without life there is no age.

Should you not live through the
hard, the candy would not taste
sweet.

We endure the cold before we get
to enjoy the warmth.

Don't get too cozy
Mother Nature has a wicked sense
of humor.

Loving hard, luminous and crying
like a heathen.

Void

We can see everything.
Even, if we're not looking.

We've seen Hell in a train station;
or in that town where everything
has changed, but still stayed the
same.

We remember visiting Heaven;
when we heard that song from the
past, felt like an old friends hug.

We've been in Limbo like desk job;
time fleeing in a world full of
immortals, folks who consume to
feel young.

We heard the Void calling; voices
of killed Mentors crying to come
back.

Save the kind from "him".

V

Don't panic

MONEY

Children are raised with money.

The mindset screams, that only
the biggest asshole, that fucking
programmed robot, is the one
who's gonna make it.

The real story is a love story;
maybe it got a bit tragicomic at the
end.

THAT MAN

Brown hair all messed up, side,
down.

Deodorant, then a blouse in the
floor, the black jeans are inside
out, I pick pieces one by one.

They confuse when you smile.
Ignore when you cry, so I try and
walk a line, I listen tracks one by
one.

I hold on to my green bag,
every time I see that same man,
like it was the last day on the
planet.

I remember gods one by one.
Let's not start about that, man.

SLOW DOWN

Human condition: the hunger to
learn; shape and create.

There is a reason why people in
big cities walk faster than people
in a small towns.

Nature doesn't hurry.
We shouldn't either.

Why do I have to rush through
life?

Maybe the biggest lesson yet to
learn is to slow down.

CREDITS

Borderline crazy credits; the soul
is spent and the payments are
overdue.

Tremors of the heart; fighting for a
never ending Fight.

Mind's flickering like a used
cigarette lighter and just as it
ignites illusions

You wake up, start again
Try and build a life.

THE MACHINES ARE NOT RUNNING

The streets are empty now.
Emotions are gone and everything
is forbidden.

Phones are not ringing and the
machines are not running.

It started with riots and envious
rights, out of spite.

People started to make plans
and everybody was standing on
chaos, they did it.

Erased feelings and uploaded
them in to a cloud.

The streets are empty now.

WORDSMITH

I am just a wordsmith.
No; I don't wanna hit you.
True I am trying.

Sometimes I think I am dying;
Only few times it's felt like flying,
thousand and hundred hours
spent crying.

No more, I said, I started fighting;
loving the days and nights in this
fast life; forever fleeing.

SUMMERTIME

Jump to the dream pool; night
time revenants are playing sweet
dark tunes.

There no fog or a graveyard; the
welcome card announces they're
good delusions.

No screams or fear; in the summer
there's only beer, ice scream and
godly cheers.

Jump to the pool.

SENSES

I read you like an unforgettable
book.

I listen to you like my favorite
record.

I smell you like a bee smells
flowers.

I taste your lips like I was biting an
apricot.

I look at you like a tourist looks at
Grand Canyon.

I remember you like a photo,
trapped in moments.

DEBT

Oh this is not the way
It was meant to enfold.

If you are a humanoid in this
planet earth, you will come to
know that everything has a price.

You need money for everything.
Either you consume or not.

Maybe you'll even need debt, but
you should remember, love
doesn't cost a thing.

And you are not in debt.
Unconditional love means you are
free, free to love.

We can't all get along but we all
love something, live for the thing.

You love.

(UN)BELIEVER

This isolation made me believe in
anything and nothing.

Made me question and ponder
Turned me upside down.

Everything is possible and
nothing really matters.

No wonder God left,
He's as lonely as the next.

ALTERED

Vampire life is not immutable or
set, as are you; we are altered
not only by blood, but by
education and experience.

Years roll and you become more
motivated towards books and
culture.

Hardest thing I see in every
revenant, human or vampire
altered is adapting to the never
ending change.

You change in looks and your
mind changes too.

Only going forward
I hope, fear is evicted, maybe we
can finally fix the heart broken
too.

CUP OR A MUG

A tea cup, that wants to be a coffee
mug with milk and two sugars.

Problems no one cared about.

She was all flowers and no guns,
rock 'n' roll & coffee; instead of tea
& biscuits.

Lost generation; war time mug,
numb and could not get anything
done.

Until a young man, new face in this
land, played rock and drank from
that forgotten cup.

LAST STEP

Here is the last grain of sand from
my pocket.

Last step before I paralyze
completely.

The last sentence in a long letter
The last minute of the hour

I have fallen and I am ready to give
up.

I lay bloody on ripped white
feathers.

Everything is burning around me
A sharp light blue sky above me
The brown ground beneath me

Here is; my last breath.

IN THE PARK WITH YOU

I used to walk in park with you,
usually stopped there, just to
smell the air.

Now when I go there, everything is
gray, no colours left anywhere.

I couldn't keep you there, you left
but I still look for you everywhere
I promise, I'll find you after I'm
dead.

HIGHWAY

We are all traveling in the age of
wisdom, on an information
highway.

To think there is no common
sense left, I'm scared.

It aired on the radio, everybody
knows everything now.

How all feels petrified and fearful,
but don't show you that.

Strip down all knowledge and be
stupid with me.

PAST THE PLEASURE ZONE

To taste it countless times; no, it's not chocolate, all though it's good.

I think it's not edible all though, it could be experienced through food.

Je t'aime vie.

Life is my passion; past any pleasure zone and in all of them.

BAR FIGHT

They were banned from the bar
and it made us drop our jaws, at
least over flow our pints.

In that night when the Sea and the
Thunder got into a fight

I remember the rumble and the
shouts

It turns out, the Sea now only
drinks wine with poets and newly-
weds

Thunder gets just a half of a pint.

SOUL IS NO OBJECT

Soul can feel like a demon
if you don't get to know what it
wants

See it carries a lot of stuff

all those alien tentacles gripping
tight

this splattered ink full of
memories

Sentimental road ahead and the
path you are walking now

Will I ever know what it wants or
needs to see from the past,
present and the future all at once?

7.1 OF A HUMAN

I am one of them,
Then I think what am I
Try to join them

No, no, no.

No one's together anymore
really they walk alone
under the neon lights

No, no, no.

Searching for community
this silence isn't golden anymore
really 7.1 billion people are alone

No, no, no.

LETTERS FROM LONELINESS

More than anything, he wants to
swim.
I'm with him when he dives in.

Vessel trapped in the time stream.
He just thinks it's a dream.
Man wakes up in his bed.

Ends up fighting with me

He knows that if someone saw
how crazy it must seem, him
shouting alone to his bedroom
wall.

All together in the end from the
loneliness, he found solitude and I
was his friend.

FIRE SIGNIA

Some men want to watch the
world burn

Turns out I am not that kind of
pyromaniac

Different, nice and kind slow
burning fire

Really playful flame and ice cold
tongue

Hit the heart Kong that sings OM

My fuel is love and I set the path
on fire.

THESE WORDS

I have these words I need to say.
There's no other way.

Say what's in my heart, mind, body
and soul.

You'll know that I can't apologize.

This fire and ice inside the pupils
on my eyes

These words I need to say.

THIS BOOK IS DEDICATED TO MY
FAMILY, FRIENDS AND READERS.

THANK YOU ANNIKA, HARRI, JUHA,
JUHANI, JANET, LAURA, MARJO, ROLF
AND RAIJA.

THANK YOU ALL FOR YOUR LOVING
SUPPORT.

CONTENT

I FICTION MADE REALITY

II SHAMEFUL MYSTICISM

III MAGICAL FIRES

IV Sunny times in void

V DON'T PANIC

I TAKE A BATH WITH FEAR.

ALL OF THEM FIERY
BUBBLES POPPING AGAINST
MY SKIN.

DON'T PANIC.